MASTODON

PREHISTORIC BEASTS
MASTODON

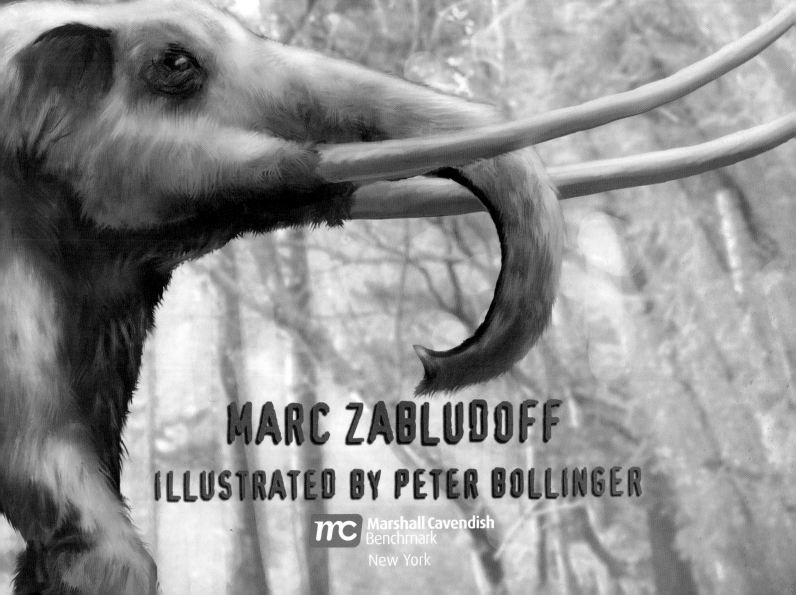

MARC ZABLUDOFF
ILLUSTRATED BY PETER BOLLINGER

Marshall Cavendish
Benchmark

New York

Published by Marshall Cavendish Benchmark
An imprint of Marshall Cavendish Corporation

Other Marshall Cavendish Offices: Marshall Cavendish International (Asia) Private Limited, 1 New Industrial Road, Singapore 536196 • Marshall Cavendish International (Thailand) Co Ltd. 253 Asoke, 12th Flr, Sukhumvit 21 Road, Klongtoey Nua, Wattana, Bangkok 10110, Thailand • Marshall Cavendish (Malaysia) Sdn Bhd, Times Subang, Lot 46, Subang Hi-Tech Industrial Park, Batu Tiga, 40000 Shah Alam, Selangor Darul Ehsan, Malaysia

Marshall Cavendish is a trademark of Times Publishing Limited

All websites were available and accurate when this book was sent to press.

Library of Congress Cataloging-in-Publication Data

Zabludoff, Marc.
Mastodon / Marc Zabludoff ; illustrated by Peter Bollinger.
p. cm.—(Prehistoric beasts)
Summary: "Explore Mastodon, its physical characteristics, when and where it lived, how it lived, what other animals lived alongside it, and how we know this"—Provided by publisher.
Includes bibliographical references and index.
ISBN 978-1-60870-036-3
1. Mastodons—North America—Juvenile literature. I. Title.
QE882.P8Z329 2011
569'.67—dc22
2010002508

Editor: Christine Florie
Publisher: Michelle Bisson
Art Director: Anahid Hamparian
Series Designer: Alicia Mikles

Photo research by Connie Gardner

The photographs in this book are used by permission and through the courtesy of:
Getty Images: Marvin E. Newman, 9; *AP Photo*: Steve Mitchell, 18; *Photo Researchers*: Spencer Sutton, 21.

Printed in Malaysia (T)
135642

CONTENTS

MEALTIME FOR MASTODONS

In a dense forest of evergreens a group of elephant-like creatures is noisily eating. Animals throughout the forest can hear the sounds of branches cracking, the thud of heavy footsteps, and the constant crackle of big teeth chewing wood and leaves.

The biggest animal in the group, a thirty-year-old female, looks like a furry, reddish brown hill against the deep green of the trees surrounding her. Lifting her long trunk over her head, she grabs a branch of a spruce tree, bends it against her broad, curving tusks, and snaps it off. Casually, she pulls the branch through her mouth, stripping off the delicious needles and cones.

One of the smaller animals, an energetic two-year-old, starts honking loudly as he looks up at a cluster of cones too high for him to reach. A nearby adult, the youngster's aunt, lumbers over to help. Reaching up,

Mastodons once thrived in the broad, dense forests of ancient North America.

she snatches the treats with the tip of her trunk and passes them down to the little one's open mouth. As soon as he has finished eating, he decides to amble over to a pond for a dessert of water lilies. His aunt follows close behind, keeping an eye on him.

Eleven thousand years from now these giants will exist only as a display in a museum. A sign will identify their bones as those of *Mammut americanum*, the **extinct** mastodon. The thick evergreen forests in which they now wander so peacefully will be gone. In their place the land that has not been cleared for houses and farms will be woods filled with maple, oak, and birch trees.

In the fall thousands of people will drive north from nearby New York City to gaze on spectacular curtains of red and yellow as the leaves turn color. Few of them will stop to think that the land they are driving through once offered a spectacle far more fabulous.

HOW TO LOOK LIKE A MASTODON

Once upon a time North America was elephant country. Roaming across the cold North were **woolly mammoths**—shaggy beasts with enormous twisting tusks. Ruling over the plains of the South and West were their larger cousins, the 12-foot-tall Columbian mammoths. But spread across the forests of the Midwest and the East were the mastodons, in some ways the least known of all these wonderful animals.

To get an idea of just how big a mastodon was, just take a look at today's African elephant. It is a bit taller, but not as long as a mastodon.

The American mastodon stood 8 to 10 feet high at the shoulder, which is a little shorter than an African elephant. It was longer, though—some 15 feet from head to tail. It would have completely filled an average-size room in any modern house, and it probably

9

would have burst through the ceiling. Its tusks would have shot right through the walls. They were roughly 8 feet long and gently curved, first outward and then back inward.

Even if the mastodon could somehow squeeze inside that room, it would put a serious strain on the floor. An adult mastodon could weigh as much as 6 tons—12,000 pounds—about the weight of six medium-size cars.

Mastodons were covered with hair that ranged from gray to reddish or dark brown. Although they were fairly furry compared with elephants, they were not as shaggy as woolly mammoths. Their tusks were not as dramatic as a mammoth's, either, though they were longer and more curved than an elephant's.

Like mammoths, mastodons probably had small, very un-elephant-like ears. Otherwise, mastodons looked quite different from their relatives. They were bulkier and wider but shorter. They had foreheads that slanted straight back, while mammoths had domed foreheads. Mastodons also had straighter backs—a mammoth's back sloped down toward its hips. Finally, mastodons carried their heads lower and more forward so that their trunks pointed outward more than downward.

What differences and similarities can you find between a mastodon (left) and a woolly mammoth (right)?

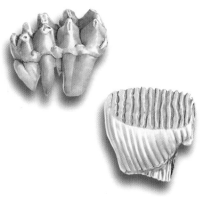

Mastodon teeth (left) were well suited for crushing and snapping twigs, leaves, and bark. The ridges on the teeth of woolly mammoths (right) helped them grind up tough plains grasses.

The biggest difference, though, was their teeth. Mammoths, like today's elephants, had huge, blocky **molars**, or cheek teeth, whose surfaces were covered with a series of ridges, like a washboard. These teeth were great for grinding up tough grasses. Mastodons, however, had molars with six to eight pairs of cone-shaped bumps on them, like tiny mountain ranges. These teeth were not very good for grinding grass, but they were excellent for clipping and crushing twigs, leaves, bark, and other parts of trees and shrubs. Unlike mammoths, mastodons were most at home in the forest, not on the plains. They preferred forests filled with evergreens and dotted with lakes and marshes.

11

A PARADE OF ELEPHANTS

Mastodons, mammoths, and modern elephants are all members of a group of animals called **proboscideans**, or animals with trunks. The first proboscideans appeared in northern Africa about 55 million years ago. They hardly looked like elephants. They were pig-size, and they had no trunks. They did have small, hippolike tusks.

Over millions of years these animals **evolved**, or changed. They grew much larger, for starters. Their tusks, which began as front teeth, turned outward and grew longer. Their legs grew much thicker. Most remarkably, their nose and upper lip fused, or joined together, to form a long, flexible trunk that allowed them to reach food and water on the ground without bending down.

Gradually, the **descendants** of these animals spread out from Africa and into Europe and Asia. Over thousands of centuries as many as 160 distinct kinds, or **species**, of proboscideans appeared. Many had two tusks

Mastodons, mammoths, and elephants evolved from smaller proboscideans.   13 on their upper jaws, as elephants do today. But many others had two more tusks on their lower jaws as well. Among them were strange-looking animals known as shovel tuskers, which had two lower tusks that were flattened into spadelike digging tools. Other species had lower tusks that turned downward, toward the ground.

Some proboscideans evolved into animals called shovel tuskers. Their lower tusks looked like digging tools.

Mastodons appeared millions of years before the mammoths and the "true" elephants did. But they were not the ancestors of these other animals. They were cousins, and rather distant cousins at that.

By 15 million years ago the mastodons had made it to North America, walking across a bridge of land that then existed between Siberia and Alaska. It was there that the most famous member of the mastodon family, the American mastodon, appeared, close to 4 million years ago.

Like elephants, mastodons probably lived in family groups made up of youngsters and adult females.

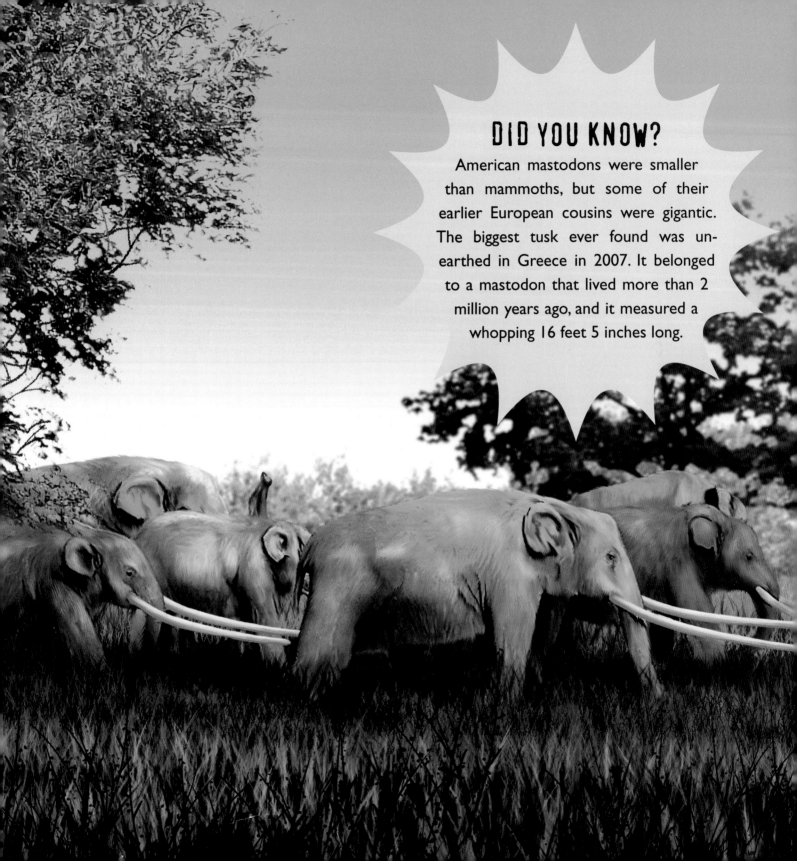

DID YOU KNOW?
American mastodons were smaller than mammoths, but some of their earlier European cousins were gigantic. The biggest tusk ever found was unearthed in Greece in 2007. It belonged to a mastodon that lived more than 2 million years ago, and it measured a whopping 16 feet 5 inches long.

MASTODONS IN NORTH AMERICA

Even during the Ice Age, when Earth grew colder and thick slabs of ice covered the northern part of North America, the mastodons thrived. South of the ice the country was green, and temperatures were cool. Evergreen forests of spruce, cedar, and pine trees carpeted huge stretches of land. There were thousands of ponds and swamps in which a hungry mastodon could feed on moss and water plants.

Scientists have found hundreds of mastodon **fossils**—preserved bones, tusks, and teeth—all over the United States. At various times the North American mastodon lived nearly everywhere on the **continent**, from Alaska to Mexico and Florida, from California to New York. Some of its favorite spots were apparently along the East Coast and around the Great Lakes.

Mastodons made their homes south of the frigid northern glaciers in areas that were green with lush vegetation.

This mastodon skeleton was discovered in Palm Beach County, Florida, in 1969.

Yet despite the abundance of fossils, scientists still do not know as much about mastodons as they do about woolly mammoths. There are two reasons for this. First, because woolly mammoths lived in the far north, some of them became frozen soon after they died. Their frozen bodies were preserved for thousands of years. Thanks to these mammoth mummies, **paleontologists** know the size and shape of body parts that do not normally become fossils, like ears. We have no frozen mastodons, however, and so we are not certain about details such as these.

WHERE AND WHEN WAS THE FIRST MASTODON FOSSIL FOUND?

A fist-size mastodon tooth was discovered in 1705 in Claverack, New York, in the Hudson River valley. But no one knew what the strange object was. Many people thought it was a human tooth, evidence that a tribe of giants had once lived in North America. American Indians had also found mastodon teeth and bones, but they too thought the fossils came from giants.

The second reason we know more about woolly mammoths than mastodons is that people—the "cavemen" of Ice Age Europe—left us wonderfully precise paintings on cave walls of these animals. They left no pictures of mastodons, however, because they never saw them. European mastodons disappeared 2 million years before artistic humans arrived in the area. The first people in North America must have seen mastodons roaming the forests. But if they painted or carved any clear pictures of the animals, we have yet to find them.

Cave drawings of woolly mammoths give us a lot of information about these ancient beasts.

LIFE AMONG THE TUSKERS

Like today's elephants, mastodons lived long lives—sixty years or so—but they took a long time to grow up. Male mastodons did not become adults until they were at least ten years old. Females took even longer to mature.

Scientists believe mother mastodons watched over their young for many years.

This means that a mastodon youngster depended on its mother's care for many years. It also means that a mother mastodon often had more than one or two demanding youngsters to look after at a time. So the mother, in turn, depended on the help of other adults to raise her big babies.

The mother also needed their help in protecting her family. No meat-eating **predators**, not even wolves or terrifying **saber-toothed cats**, would risk attacking a full-grown mastodon. But they would seize a young mastodon if given a chance. As a result, mastodons lived in groups. The group could be as small as five or six animals or as large as thirty or forty. But it was most likely made up entirely of adult

Though fierce hunters, saber-toothed cats did not attempt to attack adult mastodons.

females—all sisters or cousins, mothers or daughters—and any number of youngsters, both male and female. The young females probably stayed with the group for their entire lives. The males, though, probably went off to live on their own when they grew up.

Male mastodons were not very good at getting along with others. From markings on fossil tusks and skulls, paleontologists have concluded that male mastodons fought with one another frequently. Most likely, they fought over the females.

Those fights could be vicious. Today, male elephants battle by smashing their trunks or tusks together or by pushing against each other, head to head. Mastodon fights could be a lot more deadly. Evidently, the males would use their long, curving tusks to stab rivals in the neck or head.

DID YOU KNOW?

Like elephants, mastodons favored one tusk over the other. An individual mastodon could be either a right-tusker or a left-tusker, but some evidence suggests most were lefties.

It was not unusual for male mastodons to fight one another over a female mastodon.

END OF THE LINE

A mastodon living in Ice Age North America could generally look forward to a good, long life.

Unfortunately for the great beasts, North America ultimately became a much less comfortable home than it once had been. One of the biggest changes came with the arrival of humans. Although they had long lived in the rest of the world, humans did not arrive in North America until around 11,000 years ago, near the end of the Ice Age. With their stone-tipped weapons, these human hunters were the first predators able to threaten an animal as big as an adult mastodon.

A much greater danger may have been posed by the changing **climate**. As the Ice Age ended and Earth became warmer, the mastodons' forest home began to shrink. Eventually, this meant that more and more animals were competing for less and less food. The big mastodons must have found

With the coming of humans and a change in climate, mastodons became extinct about ten thousand years ago.

TO SURVIVE, COULDN'T MASTODONS HAVE GONE NORTH, WHERE IT WAS COOLER?

Temperature was not really the problem—mastodons had lived for thousands of years in Florida, for instance. The problem was the lack of a proper home. The North had been covered with ice for ages, and the evergreen forests the mastodons needed to survive would not start to grow there for another thousand years.

it especially hard to survive. They were destructive eaters, tearing up big areas of forest. As long as there was plenty of forest, they could keep moving to new feeding spots while the old ones regrew. Now though, that became impossible.

The youngest mastodons would have been in the most danger. The same is true of elephants today—when there is not enough food the young elephants die before the adults. If conditions improve, the number of animals can increase again. But for the mastodons, conditions did not improve. With fewer babies living to become adults and with hunters on the lookout for any survivors, the days of the mastodon came to an end. By ten thousand years ago North America had become a land without elephants.

TIMELINE

55 million years ago	Proboscideans, or animals with trunks, appear in North Africa.
35 million years ago	Mastodons' ancestors appear.
20 million years ago	Mastodons spread across Europe.
15 million years ago	Mastodons arrive in North America.
6 million years ago	Ancestors of the "true" elephants appear in Africa.
2 million years ago	Mastodons become extinct in Europe.
1.8 million years ago	Earth's climate begins to cool, and a series of ice ages begins.
100,000 years ago	The last Ice Age begins.
20,000 years ago	The Ice Age peaks, with great ice sheets covering North America as far south as Wisconsin.
15,000 years ago	Earth begins to warm.
12,000 years ago	The ice sheets begin to melt.
10,000 years ago	Mastodons, along with many other large Ice Age mammals, go extinct.

GLOSSARY

climate	the average kind of weather in a particular place over a long time period.
continent	any one of the seven great bodies of land on Earth: North America, South America, Europe, Asia, Africa, Australia, and Antarctica.
descendants	all of an animal's offspring: its children, grandchildren, and so on.
evolve	to change over time.
extinct	gone forever.
fossil	the remains of an animal or plant that lived thousands or millions of years ago.
molar	one of the large grinding teeth in the back of the mouth.
paleontologist	a scientist who studies fossils to learn about life from the past.
predator	an animal that hunts and eats other animals.
proboscideans	the group of animals that have trunks, such as mastodons, mammoths, and elephants.
saber-toothed cat	an extinct Ice Age meat eater that had two long, pointed canine teeth in the upper jaw, which it used to kill other animals.
species	a particular kind of plant or animal, different from all others.
woolly mammoth	an extinct, hairy proboscidean and a distant cousin of the mastodon.

28

FIND OUT MORE

Books

Kumin, Maxine. *Mites to Mastodons: A Book of Animal Poems*. New York: Houghton Mifflin, 2006.

Morrison, Taylor. *Mastodon Mystery*. New York: Houghton Mifflin, 2006.

Sabuda, Robert and Matthew Reinhart. *Encyclopedia Prehistorica: Mega-Beasts*. Cambridge, MA: Candlewick Press, 2007.

Zabludoff, Marc. *Woolly Mammoth*. New York: Marshall Cavendish Benchmark, 2010.

Websites

The Mastodon Project

www.priweb.org/mastodon/mastodon_home.html

The Mastodon Project: The Paleontological Research Institute has worked with Cornell University on unearthing several mastodons in upstate New York. This site shows how the fossils are dug out and preserved, and how kids have helped with the work.

The Thomas Jefferson Fossil Collection

www.ansp.org/museum/Jefferson/mastodon/index.php

The Academy of Natural Sciences in Philadelphia houses many fossils once owned by Thomas Jefferson, among which are teeth and bones of mastodons. Its website offers pictures and extensive information about mastodon history for curious parents and children alike.

INDEX

Page numbers in **boldface** are illustrations.

ABOUT THE AUTHOR

Marc Zabludoff, the former editor in chief of *Discover* magazine, has been involved in communicating science to the public for more than two decades. His other work for Marshall Cavendish includes books on spiders, beetles, and monkeys for the AnimalWays series, along with books on insects, reptiles, and the largely unknown and chiefly microscopic organisms known as protoctists. Zabludoff lives in New York City with his wife and daughter.

ABOUT THE ILLUSTRATOR

Peter Bollinger is an award-winning illustrator whose clients include those in the publishing, advertising, and entertainment industries. Bollinger works in two separate styles, traditional airbrush and digital illustration. He lives in California with his wife, son, and daughter.